Ashore

Tupelo Press
North Adams,
Massachusetts

PREVIOUS WINNERS OF THE
TUPELO PRESS FIRST / SECOND BOOK AWARD:
THE BERKSHIRE PRIZE

ANNA MARIE HONG, *Fablesque*
Selected by Aimee Nezhukumatathil

ELIZAABETH ACEVEDO, *Medusa Reads La Negra's Palm*
Selected by Gabrielle Calvocoressi

PATRICK COLEMAN, *Fire Season*
Selected by Carol Frost

JENNY MOLBERG, *Marvels of the Invisible*
Selected by Jeffrey Harrison

AMY MCCANN, *Yes, Thorn*
Selected by Paisley Rekdal

KRISTINA JIPSON, *Halve*
Selected by Dan Beachy Quick

YE CHUN, *Lantern Puzzle*
Selected by D.A. Powell

MARY MOLINARY, *Mary & the Giant Mechanism*
Selected by Carol Ann Davis and Jeffrey Levine

DANIEL KHALASTCHI, *Manoleria*
Selected by Carol Ann Davis and Jeffrey Levine

MEGAN SNYDER-CAMP, *The Forest of Sure Things*
Selected by Carol Ann Davis and Jeffrey Levine

JENNIFER MILITELLO, *Flinch of Song*
Selected by Carol Ann Davis and Jeffrey Levine

KRISTIN BOCK, *Cloisters*
Selected by David St. John

DWAINE RIEVES, *When the Eye Forms*
Selected by Carolyn Forché

LILIAS BEVER, *Bellini in Istanbul*
Selected by Michael Collier

DAVID PETRUZELLI, *Everyone Coming Toward You*
Selected by Campbell McGrath

BILL VAN EVERY, *Devoted Creatures*
Selected by Thomas Lux

AIMEE NEZHUKUMATATHIL, *Miracle Fruit*
Selected by Gregory Orr

JENNIFER MICHAEL HECHT, *The Last Ancient World*
Selected by Janet Holmes

From the waters of Waikīkī, to the forests outside Honolulu, and across the Pacific ocean, the poems in Laurel Nakanishi's debut collection consider the relationships between place and story. In estrangement and intimacy, at home and away, on the surface and in the depths, these poems level a steady gaze on the world and ask, "And yet, what do I really know?" The answer comes in memory and geography, in old songs and moments folded into a larger time. These poems ask us to live deeply on the earth, to attend to the "stories at work in us," and know ourselves anew.

"*Ashore* is an elegant, incisive, and formally restive meditation, a meditation — born of juxtaposition — on life's incongruencies: the myth of O'ahu as an 'island / that sleeps on the ocean floor, a great mountain / rising to break the surface' beside the island's capitalist reality of 'the stretch of sidewalk / from Kam Shopping Center to the Nu'uanu McDonalds,' all of this beside yet another reality, namely, the island's sheer natural beauty. The poems here pitch place against placelessness, family against estrangement, island life against the so-called mainland of the United States. They consider how race — being of mixed race, in particular — both contains and enacts all of these conundrums, how race itself is a conundrum, just as colonization is — colonization as old as nature itself apparently, given how 'Moss has colonized the road / in green islands.' I admire the attention of these poems, as I admire throughout the collection a steady note of joy that seems all the more persuasive because the poems don't flinch from what is joyless — where would one be, they ask, without the other?" — *From the Judge's Citation by Carl Phillips*

Ashore

Laurel Nakanishi

Library of Congress LCCN: 2020949829
ISBN-13: 978-1-946482-51-8

Cover art "Words" by Solomon Enos. Used by permission of the artist.

Cover and text design by Kenji Liu.

First paperback edition March 2021

Tupelo Press
P.O. Box 1767
North Adams, Massachusetts 01247
(413) 664-9611 / Fax: (413) 664-9711
editor@tupelopress.org / www.tupelopress.org

Tupelo Press is an award-winning independent literary press that publishes fine fiction, non-fiction, and poetry in books that are a joy to hold as well as read. Tupelo Press is a registered 501(c)(3) non-profit organization, and we rely on public support to carry out our mission of publishing extraordinary work that may be outside the realm of the large commercial publishers. Financial donations are welcome and are tax deductible.

This project is supported in part by an award from the National Endowment for the Arts.

TABLE OF CONTENTS

For you, beloved islands, beloved earth

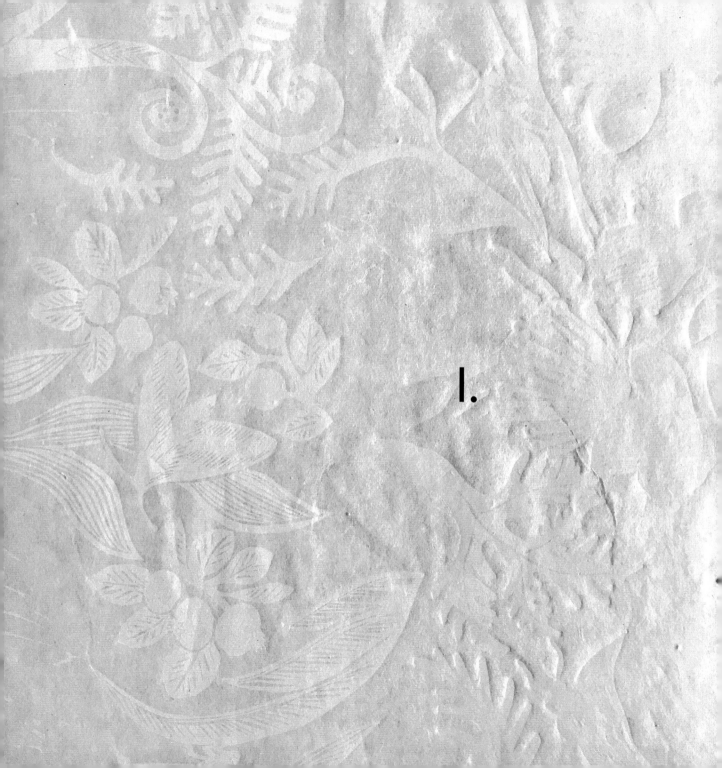

I.

INVOKING THE BODHISATTVAS' NAMES IN HONOLULU

Bodhisattva of the other shore. Bodhisattva
of the sweet come sweeping hand.
Bodhisattva of salt and small places —
                              of Kalihi, Kapālama, Liliha.

At the corner of School and Houghtailing St.,
Burt-guys pump gas and lean into engines.
On Kuakini St., incense hangs
          above the sidewalk like words just beyond hearing.
Head 'Ewa and you'll find Puea cemetery choking
with high grass, hiding the grave
of Joseph Kahahawai Jr.
              "Born Dec. 25, 1909, Killed Jan. 8, 1932"

Island of asphalt and sun glut,
                    blinkered in tinted glass. Downtown crouches
at the water's edge and we tread the churned up
burial grounds of someone's parents.
Whose?

Come Tahiti Come Chuuk
Come China   Come Samoa   Who?
Come Japan   Come Korea
Come Philippines   Come Americas   Who?
Come Portagees   Come Micros
Come Buddha-heads   Come Haoles

Whose eyes reached back into Kalihi Valley
and said: "Paradise." Or they said,
                              "Good enough."
Or maybe they called out the names of their children —
those yet to be born, those they would plant here.
Wellspring, fecundity, the valley held them
          and the car-lined streets and the houses piled
                too close up the ridge-side.

Bodhisattva of the tents and shopping carts
on the grassy median by River Street — show us
the shining haired children who duck
                              amongst the slanting clotheslines.

Bodhisattva of old Kalihi Hospital,
              show us the graves of the lepers who were taken
from their families, forced into quarantine,
                                             and died there.

Bodhisattva of pau hana traffic and those six lanes
of idling cars on H1 — allow us a glimpse
of the green-faced Koʻolau, that backbone of our island.

Our island that sleeps
                         on the ocean floor, a great mountain
rising to break the surface. All we know is the summit.
All we know is the stretch of sidewalk
from Kamehameha Shopping Center to the Nuʻuanu McDonalds.

And the shanks, and the blades,
and that drug-laden loping walk — All we know
is the rumble of buses, the letters that peel from signs.

In the heat of the afternoon
kids walk home in packs, sweating through their
uniforms, brown arms swinging.
                                Bodhisattva of their arms.

Bodhisattva of their dark hair and long limbed walk.
Bodhisattva of that walk —
soothe their sidelong glances, their rabbit-quick hearts.

May they arrive at the other shore, at the sweet hand,
at that small place: a breath
                                between the dusk and rising night.

MĀNOA

HAUNT :
There were stories at work in us — night marchers with their spears and their shark-toothed clubs. The mist, a sistering hand over our eyes; she fell upon us. We dared each other along. We made it as far as the stream where the tree ferns, where the trail drops to a ravine full of broken glass. It was no place for night.

HIDING :
Or that night we stayed too late and your father came searching, stroking the forest with his flashlight. We watched him pass and ran home.

PHOTOGRAPH :
Crouched on a boulder, you still have hair. It is blown to one side. The waterfall dissolves to mist on impact. It has fogged your half-smile, your hands pointing two-fingered as they did in gesture. Your knees are wet and streaked by mossrocks; we had clambered to this place. Everything falls short of this moment.

WAR GAMES

There is a war at school   You are not sure how it began
                                    Everyone is carrying rocks

    The lines are so clearly drawn
that you find yourself on the gutter-behind-the-kickball-field team
      without even trying   Mariko   whose name
always reminded you of some percussive instrument
                    is pointing out the weakness in the enemy's defense

This is a rock-throwing war

all of their pockets bulge   Nic holds a big one
in both hands   At some point the rocks are thrown
They must be

Then you go home   you clean up   you twirl spaghetti
          All that time the rock you threw
is still in the air   It is arcing over third base

it is ten paces from the soft foreheads of the enemy   It is spinning slightly
          still warm from your palm

MY BROTHER, IN EIGHT PANELS

1. They say he looks foreign, my brother. They say he steams kale. They say he eats as he walks: lunch hour, shoving a burrito into his mouth. They avoid saying hello at these times. They say he never wants to return home. Was it the sun pouring into his cement-walled room all through our childhood? They say he is happy with the distance that oceans make.

2. With the distance that oceans make, over the remains of a dinner that we have eaten too quickly, in a B-rate Malaysian restaurant, we try for a pleasant conversation: work, his dog, cellphones, media, his dog again. He slouches back into his chair, jabbing the table with the tip of his *hashi*. I've leaned back too. The waiter brings another pot of tea. For a moment, we both watch steam rise from the spout.

3. Steam rises from the spout of Grandma's teapot. My brother ducks under the table and scoots past the tangle of chair legs. I follow, bowing "*Gochisosama!*" and race after him. In the yard: "Look, that tree has sprouted pennies," he says, plucking a coin from the bark crease. "Wow, a dime!" I call, pointing to where I had wedged it just that morning. It is a fine trick. We search the bark until the night comes shuttering our eyes. My brother pats the trunk and says, "Thank you, money tree." I marvel at his gullibility. He walks away jangling pockets full of my change.

4. With pockets full of our father's money, we make for the pier. We are not elegant, but I have just emerged from my first year of college, so we will eat in the finest restaurant in town. The Puget Sound makes quiet waves. "If you only had twelve hours to live," he says, "I would take you to meet this famous poet. I don't read that stuff, but most people know of her."
   "I suppose that is when poetry matters most," I say. "And what would you do? If you only had twelve hours?"
   "I would tell off everyone who has been an asshole to me."
   We watched each other over the cutlery.

5. We watch; we are each other's keeper of time, of those past selves running through the bamboo forest or catching guppies with green nets. Somewhere still we are marching through the house singing the *appleskin* song. We are mid-summer, scratching rock drawings. When I say that I don't know him, it's not true. And yet, what do I really know?

6. What do I really know? At sixteen he took a pickax and swung it high above his head. Swung it unskillfully, but with strength. His arms were too long for his body then. The pickax made a great arc before coming down on the money tree. Its branches snapped too easily, so he bludgeoned a boulder, the one I thought looked like a dinosaur's head. He hit it again and again, gouging white dust from the rock.

7. From the rock, from the crucible of deadline and fever-stress, my brother shapes his genius. From catastrophe, from breach, from the buzz of almost-ruin, my brother plucks just the right words. How he works. How he works. "Hi. sorry can't talk at work." Years of silence, then just the right words, thrown down to me like crumbs: "I'm proud of you. I hope the rest of us can learn from your kind soul."

8. I hope the rest of us can learn what to do with these rinds, these scraps; I am always starving with you. Oh, my brother, my beautiful heretic, what else is left for us? This street? Its yellowing light? The corner where you chipped your tooth and I held your chin, bloody, to peer up into your hurt. Brother, I know you do not read poetry. Still the day ended here. We walked home in silhouettes, failing indigo. Porch lights flickered on. We moved deeper in, farther away, tending the silences in our own feral minds.

MĀNOA

WHAT GROWS:
A grove of hau, the greening arms and my body bending. Handhold and foothold, the moss came away. I lay nose into it and looked for a long time at the pillowheads, the curling yellow stalks, the tiny end-bulbs, so I could know just what I was destroying.

HAU:
1. Hawaiian canoe plant used for weaving rope. The fibers, even when split, are strong enough to hold the wind in sails across the Pacific.
2. The tree under which Robert Lewis Stevenson wrote poetry, Sans Souci beach, 1883, sugar cubes dissolving in his tea.
3. The thicket of secret caves where children climb and hoot at the Honolulu Zoo. They will ask you for a password. Tell them: *Tunnel in jungle gym.*

DRIVING TO THE NORTH SHORE, I IMAGINE MY BROTHER

not estranged, but there with me
as the ironwoods along the highway
lace a brief tunnel - eclipsing
the sky - then breathe us out
again. Red dirt loose
in the fields where the pineapple grew,
where sugarcane, where our grandparents
sang *hole hole bushi*:
My husband cuts the cane stalks,
And I trim the leaves —
Slipping down the hill
from Schofield Barracks to the North Shore,
the road twists. Crosses
punctuate the millage.
My brother lifts his feet
from the dashboard
and turns to look at me.
His gaze is gentle
like the folding valleys of the Waianae range.
And he is not looking at me,
but at the peaks, remembering,
perhaps, that hike to Peacock Flats —
how we barely made it, scrambling,
holding our rubber slippers
in our hands. And finally
the view from the top — the whole coastline
from Kaʻena Point to Haleiwa.
The waves breaking offshore.
The great blue welcome of horizon.
I remember it vividly — a fluke
of childhood because, in truth,
I was not there. My brother
stood alone, panting, victorious,
looking down at the patchwork island,

at the stories he wove
for a sister who would
believe anything of him.

THE PACIFIC NALAKAH

Day eight : birdshot island
>Just morning and the long caves are groaning. I've had another sighting. The mother emerged first, buoyed by the shore break. She appeared to be paddling with more flippers than noted on Tuesday. As she hauled her body up onto the beach, her skin sloshed and soothed and leapt up again with each movement. She scooted a comfortable distance and lay down her delicate face (with parrot-mouth) into the sand. Her tail and dorsal fin caught the wind, sending her skin rippling and peaking.

Day twelve : thursday
>I've counted three babies. They are quite small, about the size of my hand. I found them nestled in the black rock yard. The mother was nowhere near, so I pressed my face right up to their bodies (as still as tide pools) to take in their sticky scent.

Day nineteen : chorus
>I've noted seven distinct calls, each with its specific function. Low guttural — the mother's head emerges from the water, nostrils dilate and gasp. Sharp grunt — backing away from the mother where she suns, calling her babies — high wheeze (wavering across the salty air). Huffed squeaks — they clamber from the white water. Yap — and snapping their beaks at one another. Her skin, rolling mur — as if some creature passed beneath its surface. Whistle — the air at work in her body (running through the pipes and chambers).

Day twenty-three : counting
>Their fins multiply or retract in ratio to their contentment. Skin throws back the light in glimmering scales, each burning a tiny hole.

Day twenty-nine : hunger

The babies have not moved from their meager shade. They have not entered the water or rolled the sand from their backs (now dried syrupy). Their fins are few. The mother leaves for days at a time.

Day thirty-two : tempest

This morning I woke to roaring, the piling of waves. Bootless, I ran to where they were huddled against some roots — two shivering bodies. I scanned the shoreline, the foam pushing high, the backlap pulling my knees bent. I looked for a shadow in the wave face, surfacing, something to stand out against the blue.

Day thirty-seven : due east

She's returned with a crowd of dead sharks. I saw them rolling in the shore break, whole but for the eyes, and the mother (with her razored beak) picking out ribbons of entrails. I joined them, plucking the tender-most bits for the babies who scrabbled and flopped, opening their beaks for more.

Day forty : we linger

They sleep at all hours, especially in the afternoon. The babies have taken to napping in my boots. The mother sprawls under my canopy shade, thrush.

Day forty-four : a dream

That I had found it swimming weakly in a tide pool. I took its translucent body in my hands and blew gently into its face. It burst with fins.

MĀNOA

THE BAMBOO CLOSED ONE-INCH DOORS :
I knew you by your slipping. Those two long tracks slid into the forest.
I followed.

PHOTOGRAPH :
A pool in the stream has turned bright orange. The roots, the water, the silt. We breathed in the metallic scent, but did not touch it. For a while, we knew the world from two feet away. *Stand right there,* you said, *be my foreground.*

WAIMEA VALLEY I

The rain comes as a blessing and often -
red lehua plucked and plucked again.

Waimea valley draws us back, winding
with Kamananui stream. We are moved

into narrow places — the tender sky
between leaves, the bird chirrup

and pause. Gusts of wind loosen fruits
high in the canopy. Everything ripens

and falls. We've grown accustomed
to the rain pooling,

the cement splitting where roots lift.
Moss has colonized the road

in green islands. We walk along
the paved way right up to the pool

and water falling — Wailele
It changes as we do

sometimes *Waihī* — softly trickling, baring its rocks,
sometimes *Waiheʻe* — purging cascade.

And once it dried completely.
The stream bed cracked, the pool sunk

until we clambered over the slick rocks
at the very bottom. When the rain came

it was in torrents. It rent branches,
rooted out trees, carried finger-lengths

of twigs, coursed Waimea river ocher-thick
We all paid attention then.

The valley poured itself into the sea
We asked: What is wrong?

What is wrong?
Why are we being punished so?

THE SHARK

It was decided, I would care for the baby hammerhead in the bucket. I had to make sure there was enough water for it to breathe. At night I would play squeaky lullabies on my violin and slosh the water to remind the baby of waves, but sharks don't sleep. It grew larger, coiling around the bucket walls. It would stick its nose out the top. I never touched it — the underside of its head was all teeth. One hot day, I was in the city and I couldn't find any water. It evaporated before I had the time — before I even noticed — the shark dried to a crisp grey. I rubbed the skin off my fingers stroking its body.

As soon as I was grown, I left the city. My house was on the stormy east side of the island. The night before the hurricane, I taped all my windows with X's, and in the morning the beach was awash with sharks. On the sand, in the shallows, their eyes rolling, gnashing the air. The storm surge brought in sharks I had never seen before. All over the beach, there were men with steel poles and pick axes. It was a team effort. They held the shark down with their bodies as one man stabbed it through the head. The shark thrashed and flickered between fish and young man. His struggles had many arms.

The sand beneath the ocean was course and grey. That morning, the water was so glassy, I could see straight to the sea floor and his outline rising in the unbroken waves. The tide swirled around my hips; water tugging at my womb. Blood bloomed around me, opening small fists, dissolving metallic. He circled closer, motionless but for the fanning of his tail. I curled my toes into the sand and imagined him breathing in my blood, passing through his mouth, his gills. A fin on my calf, a glance against my thigh. His dark shape languid, revealing nothing.

The child was fully human. It slipped from me like a fish, but it had arms and legs. It wailed through a soft mouth. My relatives came in numbers. They fussed over the baby that I swaddled in pastels each morning. At night I would unwind the cloth to reveal his small back. I liked to run my hands over the line of scars, triangular incisions — a shark's jaw — in two wide arches. *Little One,* I crooned, *my little shark.*

When he turned two, I began to have dreams. One night I swam out through stingrays, a crowd of triangular fin tips. I lay my naked belly over black water. I swam shedding layers until I had reached a tense, new cord. It twanged through my body. I began to sink. My hair waved. My arms and legs were dead to me. Only my skin felt the water whooshing in all directions, over every surface. I closed my eyes and saw carcasses rolling in the surf, jutting bones, the water churned to a foaming red. When I returned home, the baby had climbed out of his crib. He sat on the floor in the light of the fridge, gumming strips of raw steak.

It shouldn't have been a surprise to me. It was there in his body: the shift and pull of tides, the salt pulse, the density of muscle just under his skin. His body was formed by waves. Yet, I didn't know for months. They said it was the same shark, at the surf break, the bay, the deep fishing waters. They said he capsized the boat and ate a leg from each man. They said he liked the sweet meat of children. We would be in the grocery store or bank when another shark attack story would erupt. My son would always listen in silence and then slouched off to the car.

II.

MIXED

I will not hide the hollow bodies of my prairie ancestors, those wrapped up in gun-smoke out where it is never really blue or cloudless. I have their muddied green eyes, their nose pinched against cold. My clothes bunch out as theirs, but I don't double-knot my apron. I have none.

And the Japanese blood? They never quite made it to America. After weeks at sea with the moon always cupped to the horizon, Japan rose steadily in their minds. It became a floating island, a nostalgia, a stubborn dream — they moved in. And there were the tofu peddlers, the *udon* shops, the bent knees and flat hands. By the time they docked in Hawai'i, they carried that floating island with them, an anchor home.

From them: my dark hair, slim neck, but no certain turn to the eyes. A love of pattern: rice then tea, the food not touching and each to its plate.

In Japan, old ladies squint into my face, searching. In Nicaragua, boys on the street wolf-whistle and call: "Hey little Chinagirl." In Montana, I'm not-quite-white, but white-enough.

I take my beggar bowl and go wandering. Strangers toss in their turns of phrase, their home food, their festival dancing. And I weave them into my hair — these trinkets and misunderstandings.

ODE FOR MY MONTANA GRANDMOTHER

At Seventeen

She was a clutch of seeds
and the sudden loamy smell
of crossing into the river basin.
She was a flower: saskatoon.
A flower: carnation
pinned to some boy's lapel.
My grandmother at dinner,
sitting down to a plate of venison.
Her fist —
a flower, pink with cold.
Her tongue —
supple as a doe's ear.

After the Stroke, She Remembers

Fawnlight, oak, roost, and den.
Fluttering in the tamarack boughs:
the word for raven and the raven.

Mid-Winter, a Lucid Moment

She peers out the window
and says, "Oh, this place."
Her memory is an azalea, uprooted.
It is the honeysuckle we press to our lips
and bite: vegetable tang
and the sweet cup.
So, I cut the engine there,
where the snow has pocked
with the brown husks of seeds.
An old haunt of hers, perhaps.
Pointing to the snow banks she says,
"Look." And I see reams of printer paper
unrolling all down the hillside, but softer,
made to love our eyes. "No," she says
and points again to the last of the beech
leaves hanging on through winter
in their own withered boats.

BITTERROOTS

What remains changeless? Not the words
that form in our mouths. Not the senses

that gust through us. The land does not blow away
as we do. Mountains rise and erode

but not like my face as it wears into wrinkles
in the same wind and rain. Delicate and fragmentary

we move on — our moments cupped inside a larger time.
The light on water makes sense to us.

The rise and fall of days make sense.
All things move and make a stillness thereby.

We love in the smallness of rock fissures,
in the flower's hypanthium — safe in the space we create.

It is enough, this tiny orbit, the spider's quivering step.

CATALOG

ANIMAL NO. 1: GRIZZLY
>She has the heavy grace of a tsunami. She moves
>as if pushing the earth out in front of her - setting down
>huge paws and then placing upon them a massive weight.
>We watched her walk through the trees until she disappeared
>in the undergrowth. She has moved into the hollow place
>our awe carved out. We carry her with us; we populate each forest
>with the memory of her mass.

ANIMAL NO. 2: HUMAN
>She is dressed in a second skin, dark blue,
>and booted. She has climbed the high stump
>of a fallen Tamarack, still frilled in lichen.
>Another girl stands before her, leaning in,
>the tips of their fingers just touch.

ANIMAL NO. 3: BUFFALO
>Such unlikely faces, wooly-horned
>and huge, suspended by dark cords of muscle.
>They are kneeling in the meadows.
>They are standing in the road, gazing out at us
>from the deep caves of their eyes.

ANIMAL NO. 4: BLACK BEAR
Awake and hungry for berries, for field mice,
for the soft greens of spring.
She walks rolling the new flesh
over her bones, a coat full of cinnamon.
She lassos the sweet grass with her tongue,
heavy with seed.

ANIMAL NO. 5: WOLF
The brazen white of her, seen then unseen.

THE SUN MOVING ACROSS THIS PARTICULAR EARTH

When you've run out of things to look at —
the ant's erratic mapping
        the water picking up and setting down
the hillside's double
            the mountains spreading alluvial fans
and your eyes fill
with rose hips   red shale   the deep of this lake

        When you've done your wondering at the dust:
how each fine layer has simplified itself into rust-tinged rock

and you've noticed the lobes of a thimbleberry
the fly's artful hands
the crinkled hair of a grizzly caught on a bark snare

When there is no light to see
contour and scale recede
        leaving you only the mammoth shadows   the peaks
as they block out the stars

LIVING AWAY

I lived in threes
eating dust   molasses   the wrong side of wonder
       I knew better   I would make that walk everyday   Reaping steps and then
losing them
         The days opened and closed like the ribs
              of some injured
panting animal   I would time my crossing over
with an intake of breath
        I was always on one side or another   I lived

reasonably enough
        Two doors down there was a widow   I was not her
        I knew some good jokes
My bedspread   my pump-soap
          my boxes of tea filmed over
          with pale laughter   I lived among others

       They wore loafers and heels   I saw their good-natured ankles
slip ever so slightly out of their shoes   I knew where to go
        There were the annexes   the new iron bar
      the lights turning to green   always
         green   That was the wonder

I lived like that — My body
        a long rope   it wound
and unwound   The days crawled away   And although I knew better
     I could not wait for the easy addition
        It had to come suddenly   stirring torrents from gutters
blowing out clumps of hair

HILLS ABOVE THE RATTLESNAKE

My grandmother asks to see her old house. We are in the neighborhood, driving through the Rattlesnake Valley. It was Grandpa who had sold the house and moved them to the nursing home. She had never wanted to leave. She is still angry and full of relentless longing. "*Please*," she says.

So, I wind up Lincoln Hills drive, knowing all the while it is a bad idea. I pull over outside their old home with its bright red door and box hedges. There is the garage where, for an entire winter, squirrels stole dog kibble and hid it in the undercarriage of her car. There is the kitchen window where she halved, then salted grapefruit. There is her old piano, still there, just visible through the hall door.

She is crying now. After a few moments, I drive away. But there is no leaving that house. And there is no homecoming.

AFTERWARDS, A WISH

We have a spring
of withered apples.
We watch the weather,
the thick, beginning
blooms.
The sun does its work
in us,
in dogwood,
in meadow.
I know that she will leave us
soon. Her body is already
crumpling in.
We sit quietly.
The light shifts orange
to blue-grey.
The dog growls in his sleep,
sleeps on.
In the dark,
I hear her ring
tap gently against
a wine glass.
I don't know what to wish
for her anymore.

III.

GIVEN

We are given to translucence
                    the inner world projected like a starmap
          and see where it's been pinned together

          I catch the bony cleft of my ankle
on the third step   but do not fall —
                    this is my general understanding of how things work:

                    the bus usually arrives
          traffic lights move from red to green
                    I can look at the high clouds   shapely with light
                                        and think *effulgence*

          Yet the world holds more furor than even god could want
                              agues   bloodlust
and the animal beyond comprehension

                    It is no wonder that some Japanese children
          refuse to leave their rooms for years
          and women in Korea

fear their anger will build into a "fire-illness"
                    Who is to say that limbs don't fall suddenly from bodies

that spirits don't slip in through the ear to possess
                    Models of the world unfold in our minds
                    and we expand to fit them all

THREE VIEWS OF O'AHU

One
: the hotels and their views   they shift as we do
turning their faces one behind the other
    we see straight to the sea floor   as if it is all right there

Two : beach
known and known

half-bodied crescent   salt-weighed
   sand washed steep to the shore
          stand of *hau* trees   stand of picnickers
          wind-blown   clinging to their plates

        One   One
        : the sea run   : the selling

Two :
I pull up tidewrack   grooved and puckered
with oysters   opening and closing   sticking out their bodies
each with twelve tiny arms

She sells opihi by the highway side
She sells postcards   suntans   beachfront
seashores   seashore   sea

Three :
    deep in the deep blood   the water in me
    grain moving against grain
    or is it the salt dense and crackling   swell pull and wake

I held that blue hand and willing   went under

WAIMEA VALLEY II

Valley of the high priests. Sacred
valley of Kahuna Nui, imagine the skill of their hands,

their knowledge — the whittled point of a spear.
Waimea, the place of refuge. Waimea alive

in pōhaku and iwi. Alive, Hale o Lono —
the temple for peace, for rain and harvest

and the soft rounding of creation. Alive,
Kuʻula shrine for fishing the eight seas

surrounding Hawaiʻi, for the seven nights
good for casting with net, hooks, lines, and spears.

Alive, Kauhale Kahiko — the many houses of Aliʻi,
loulu fronds and twine lash the intricate

network of beams. Alive, Halau Waʻa.
Alive, Pōhaku ʻAumākua. Alive, Hale Iwi

and those original loʻi walls, over 200 years old
rising up Kaluahole ridge. They tell us there was

another stream — its name forgotten, its flow
blocked somewhere deep underground.

Kalo dries on bowed stalks, the soft-veined
hearts calling out for living water.

Even in this wild abundance, I feel its absence.
It is carved in my side, hollow-webbed

and delicate as the chambers of bone.

PLACE(LESS)NESS

Six-thirty dawns in estuaries

                                    The tall grass dancing in its reflection
                                          (instances of drowning)

So little crosses from this side to that
                           already it is notching to an end

I am not worried
prairies lay down
                   in the same wind
                            the jungle teems — a hydra

         Imagine   all those you love — a city
                                abounding without thirst or rest
                       Spoons clink against cups
                                        Work has begun
I barely know how to live
                   entering days by the blue rip
(the sky through clouds)

                           The air makes bands around my neck
                              as I walk   somnolent on

WAIKĪKĪ DIPTYCH

l.
Two men in speedos lounge
under a saucer of shade cast
by a striped umbrella
neighbored by an old woman
on a beach chair, staring
absently at the sea.
A flock of tourists bobs
in the shore break, burning
in the late morning sun.
Now, one of the speedoed men
takes the old woman by the hand —
she is his grandmother.
She is wading hesitantly
into the ocean and he brings
handfuls of water
to her hip, to her shoulders —
as she had bathed him, perhaps,
when he was still small
and only hers.

11.
I am always under
the turquoise drapery
of this dream: the sea
a great plain, it's topmost
layer sweet with last night's
rain. Seaweed like bunches
of grapes along the tideline
and the kolea ruffling themselves
for lack of wind. They remind
me of the albatross five days
dead, her belly split open, leaking
bottle caps, lighters, ziplock
baggies — red, yellow shards
against her matted feathers
and bone. Remembering,
I could not bring myself
to swim out, float on my back
and claim a place in that sea full
of my own waste.

ELEGY WITH WHALE SONG

There are whales,
my dear one.
Do you see them
flinging their bodies
into the air
grooved fluke and tail —
making enormous
white rips
in the swaths of sea.
They sing hymns
from across the Pacific
where you are,
perhaps, sitting down to write,
the Bitterroot Mountains
white-dusted outside
your window.

I imagine you
not here on the beach, but
sea-bound, there
against the back of the whale
as she surfaces to breathe.
Your body, gray
against her gray skin.
She holds you for a moment
lifted above the waves
before gently
setting you back to sea.

I know,
I know that you have died.
And you are not
sitting down to write,
a glass of wine at hand.
You are sinking,
and the whales too,
farther down than I can dive,
farther still,
until all that is left
is the spume of your breath
windswept
across the skin of sea.

WAIMEA VALLEY III

I've been saving this in my mind for you —
the loulu palms with skirts of crackling leaves,

the wide net of a monkey pod tree,
the bird with a branded face and backward steps —

how she walked over the lily pads
until she sank and floated like a duck,

how bromeliads love the mango bark,
how seeds stick to the wing.

Up mauka the ridgelines crowd
with ironwood, strawberry guava and grass.

But I've been saving this in my mind —
the forest that could be. The seedlings of lama,

wiliwili, and koa cast down roots. The ʻohiʻa ʻai,
ʻohiʻa lehua, and alaheʻe reach into the sky.

They will catch the clouds above the old stream beds
and pull down the rain.

PACIFIC TRASH VORTEX

Remember the flesh wound, the miles of debris:
toothbrush, bottle cap, plastic bag bumping up against our legs.
Let's make a tide of it — everything covered with
the fine down of algae, everything rotting, sea-swollen,
pushing past its skin. And what has not sunk,
melds now: a roaming, buoying pile. The
waste must gather somewhere — Let it be here.
We will live on this island, all
plastic and never-rot. Soon, it will circle O'ahu, nudge our
shores, flank us skirt-bound in miles. This is the riddled
afterlife: the whale gone back into its blue depths and here,
bobbing, its meager apology.

KOLEA, PACIFIC GOLDEN PLOVER

Kolea
back-kneed

                                                    Kolea
                                                    sand-eyed

at the fluid edge
        Kolea
        swept high

                    Has it ever carried you away?

                        You are unlike the children in Nicaragua
                who weave
            and scatter before on-coming traffic

    You are not a metaphor
            for a daring life among elements
                You are not an element

                        not a property of motion
                            And though I played
                    a similar game watching the water mount up before me

                                    I only knew the solid ground

What is the solid ground?

Where winged do you find it?

WAIMEA VALLEY IV

We enter the valley silently, without shaking the branches.
We enter without startling. Alae ʻula watches us

from the estuary remembering the pitch nights
when the fire lived only in her. We follow

the pig trails listening for the rustle grunt
of Kamapuaʻa. In the quiet, our thoughts

are small gods, they fly above the earth.

PORTRAIT OF MY BROTHER
AS A BULWER'S PETREL

In the shadow valleys of Nihoa,
not much has taken hold —

dust, a few shrubs, and you
black among the ribs of pahoehoe.

Trade winds, the action of waves, sheer time
draw out the poverty of your world.

Left wing folded delicately over right,
you crouch in a bed of drift-worn twigs.

My brother, your feathers
catch an iridescence. I was mistaken

to say your black was a lava field
cooled to a course char. You are

the beetle's back, the magpie's wing,
the black of Pele's tears.

For you, Nihoa is not the mere
fragment of a volcano swept back to sea.

But the sea in all directions —
as far as a bird can fly

and still return by nightfall.

A HOMECOMING

summer, early morning
Mynas, Japanese white-eyes, and java sparrows, in fours and fives, hop over the
grass; sunlight touches first the sky above the Koʻolau, then the Koʻolau.

On my first trip to the continent, Oʻahu pulled away from under me, growing
smaller and smaller until it was just a green speck in a field of silvering blue. I
had never felt that our islands were small until that moment. Friends on the
continent remark, "I could never live on an island so far away. I would go crazy."
Yet, what is far? There is only the distance between noni leaves and the blue sky.

autumn night
Wind flickers the leaves of the strawberry guava tree; the rush of hot water
through pipes; my mother in the bath.

My body remembers: the incline of the highway ramp, a turn onto Naio Street
— sunken and riddled with potholes. Returning from the airport, it is too hot.
I am wearing too many layers. There is always the smell of flowers and car
exhaust. Something has always changed: a new garage, a line of papaya trees,
my father ducking through the doorway.

winter, late afternoon
Pale tide laps at Ala Moana beach; yellow hau leaves cover the sand, littered, too,
with the bones of grilled *kalbi*.

Those first nights back in my childhood home, I eat too much *arare* and cannot
bring myself to have a proper dinner. Sitting at my grandma's kitchen table
alone, I am not homesick, but I do feel a hunger for something like home.

summer morning
The heliconia have thrown down their shadows where rice birds flit; the
Koʻolau are a wall; they are a gathering basket for the clouds: catch them,
it rains.

My students ask: *What do you mean: 'Write a poem about home'?*

summer afternoon
The spongy bark of the mango trees have soaked up the rain; hau limbs are soft with tufts of moss; a banyan tree has fallen, bridging the gully downstream.

I dream that my students have come with me to the shoreline; a hard wind draws water from their eyes. They peer first at the ocean, then at me.

summer evening
When the city is tinged with orange, the ocean holds the sun like a boat sinking into its own brilliant reflection.

I tell my students: *First there is longing, then a bridge.*

MAHALO Ā NUI

Thank you for the fragments of story
that still beat around my mind,
for mangoes that drip from limbs
and we hop a little, grazing them
with our fingertips.

Thank you for the sweet meat, for the fibers
that wedge between our teeth like brittle floss.

Thank you for my shadow cast
over sawgrass, for that same ocher light
running tongues over the slash pine.
My nickname on my love's tongue: *Lila*
god's laughter.

Our silence lifting out each sleepy breath
and dreams of two-note whistles through the forest.

Thank you for green onions that sprout
from the root. And for my grandfather
who dried and kept them in an old canning jar
those years before he died. And when
my grandmother died, we made a raft of our breath —

listing, dipping, shuttering. Thank you, how we clung
to one another and did not drown.

Thank you islands. Thank you narrow spit of land
where I live. Lava rock, brackish water,
a square of lawn before every home.
Our neighbor's music reverberates
through the wall. A memory

of a school through trees. From the river
we see it: blue and white in a grove of papaya.

A child waits for us at the banks, waving

Come here. Come in.

IV.

MĀNOA

1.

I came back to see it   the veinwork of trees
            the roots holding out   ginger flowers so low to the ground —
            who would think to look there?

Turn mauka — inland   upland   a week of muddy shoes
            take University Ave. or Punahou St.   follow them
            into the wide green bowl   Mānoa   Above is Kōnāhuanui

the double peak   tallest of the Koʻolau
            I climb it   and the houses run all to the mouth
            gridwork   windows   grey roof upon roof

And they have come —   the rain and mist
            in stories they were children

                        Kauawaʻahila   Kauakiʻowao
                        the brother cliff rain   the sistering mist

They fall   snag   on the bamboo stalks   that clack
            against each other   as if some wet body were moving through
            There were days past the stream

pig trail days   Barefoot   toeing the mud
            I was often alone
            Somewhere a waterfall sounds   spray mossed the rocks

We shed our clothes and jumped   Remember
            the cold   our skin lifting from us like moth wings
            It was you. right?   The boy with the drops in his hair
                        It was our secret bridge to the banyans

the cave where the roots had thrown themselves
            Meet me there   the wet bank   the climbing
            when I return   you return   Mānoa :

59

                                                    vast and deep
                                                    the forest thick
              the valley swallowing our wet bodies

Rain and Mist were brother   sister   and only children
              How far can you run?   They hid in the high cliffs   Kōnāhuanui
              where they snared birds and ate wild fruit
                              until she flushed them from the canopies
How they fled —
              from the valley head   to Kūka'ō'ō   to the hill of rocky caves
              how they never really arrived

How they fall over us still
              Always the piling of one body
              over the other   always in the intake of breath

What holds me here in this cape of days   Birds
              wake white in the palms   The sun
              pulls me ringing like bells   Wade out —

                                        the sea is sword-tipped   pushing hipward
                                                a crowd of kicking feet

Before she came to this place
              she swam in tepid waters
                      and the light that scattered over her
took on the many backs of morning

Before the build up of flesh in darkness
              she felt the tides brush
                      Born to it   she is marked and washed
It swooshes in her veins
              she is our small shark   run-finned
                              we crowd to her mouth

                    These are the forbidden words: aloha
            paradise sun and sand coconut surfs-up luau
            grass skirt hang-10 hukilau beachfront blue
            hawaii   blue

These are the secret words:
You have aloha for all things, for everything around you.
            Putting one more strand of coconut fiber
on to the kaula he make one fast twist.
A deep and genuine reverence for life —
            living and becoming
                        a part of everything around you.
The green world below, the blue light above.

                                    I am braided deep among the coral heads
                                                    the angel fish
                        the open-mouthed eels   Anemones sway

                                    parrotfish sway   tufts
                            and rays and jellyfish sway
                                        Bite the hook
                        they say   take it in your mouth

and blood-lipped go surfacing   They've come
                those bull-mouthed
                    monsters   sea after sea wind-thrown   blinkered in eye-shard
The sun in pieces   in all directions cresting in light

Hollow   closing out   doubled   pitchy
                rise and swell   She has come

    the water heaps itself into waves
She lays her body over the board   Sea after sea   blue hills grown cliff-faced
                            She cups the water and throws it behind her
the wave pitches   picks her   I slide into its blue bowl
                    wing-footed   foam-hipped   nearly blotted

What is left of her?
A dozen ways to drown

Minnow   minnow   the whole sea
The whole wide sea   and my sundark arms

ll.

Supposed you did not grow up here
        You did not eat mochi on new year's   You did not learn
          to make sand tunnels by digging both hands until they met
                    You knew winter

You knew deciduous   You never fell
asleep in a banyan shadow
            You did not learn
                a hula for sixth-grade May Day

You didn't make out with your high school boyfriend
           at Diamond Head lookout   You have never come home to Hawai'i

The air does not lay down heavy in your lungs
          You do not wait
                at the curb for your mother's gray station wagon
                on its third lap around the airport
Suppose
          you've just stepped from the plane
                    and breathed that plumeria air
and looked on sun-drenched Waikīkī for the first time

I suppose you would have stumbled into a kind of paradise

There are stories at work in us
They hold us   wet in their mouths   I am braided deep
swimming to my eyes   From within the dark alleys — Kūhiō
                                  Beachwalk   Saratoga
there is no ocean   no mountains
The sky is cut into sheets   high glass windows

She steps in   This too is Hawai'i — the sand they ship from Australia
           This too is Hawai'i — hotels slouching at the water's edge

sea lapping it back: the concrete   the chlorine   the rebar   the lead paint
                              Stories at work in us —

                                        a collective longing for a tropical vacation

                                        dramatic mountain ranges
                                        aqua-blue bays
                                        wide sandy beaches
                                        volcanoes
                                        monster waves
                                        genuine Hawaiian
                                        aloha spirit

                                                2,000 miles from any continent

Through the airport   the island mouth
they have come   pale and floral   carrying boogie boards
        water bottles   beach bags   floating rings   plastic leis

They are walking up and down Kūhiō Ave.
Kūhiō beach   In and out of shops   They are on trollies
        on vacation   They are dining out   taking tours   taking pictures
        naps   the sights   time for the sunset

over the ocean now and see the green flash
                They are drinking maitais on the beach
        and swimming in January — It's like bath water!   They are wading out —
        dropping their keys   their sunglasses   their credit cards that sink

bobbing in the water with their 10-month-old
        they are rubbing sunscreen
                        shopping
for cellphone charms   crossing the street with the walk sign
    They are feeling the sun on their arms for the first time in months

plunging their faces into the water
        They are close enough to touch   How fragile we are really
                        coming away in each other's hands

III.

                                    Koa strands litter the ground   the canoes all carved and gone
                                        and Waikīkī is here   leaking chemicals and exhaust

                                                                                    It is ours
                                there is no leaving it   The towers stay   The highway stays

The living reefs
and the fish in those reefs and the eels and krill and turtle leave
                                                The shark leaves
Waikīkī beach under the glittering is all dead   Only wana
and triggerfish and the grainy sea floor

There were stories at work in us
        Plumeria untwisting   The rains
        that came coursing through the streambeds
        The narrow   and the one who moved through me

The mosquitos lingered   burrowed into our arms
        our sloping necks   It was you   right?   Your skin?
        We stood by   green laid up against green

The car idled   I loved that valley
        Deep in the trackless   the bamboo all slatted in my eyes
        a place among it   but nowhere I stayed

Climbing trees   we sat in the crook and mildew smell
        and never touched
        I   that is   was I alone all that time?

                                    Everywhere the ocean moves   below the surface   just under
                                my chin   Hermit crabs back into my mouth   How fragile
                                        we are — gunswish   whalesong   the union
                                        of your shoulder   I've swum as far as I could

65

She is braided deep   swimming
She is diving under the breakers
            They roll down her back   Leading the board
            in an arch   the bubbles at her nose
How she never really arrives

Oh weightless one   spool your hips in curtains of sea

                Push your bulk into the crumbling fists   the foam
If only I fell deep enough   If only I could pass the tips of never-back
long my feet into an island   that one

crouching   and to see it spring   all jungle-limbed
and water-boned   diving back into the sea —

IV.

Praise the sea and certain blue   Praise the smell of wax
          the sun blinding off windows   Praise the surfboards
          their shave-ice colors

stacked in the back of the truck   Praise the truck
          and my father driving   Praise our surf-full silence

the house-lined streets   the clink of our gate   stepping out of slippers
  the cool of the home   Praise the pot full of steaming rice

Alone with the lookout
the rain has stopped   the mist has dried
stalks and searing   our skin   the valley a boney imprint

We fell through our footprints
How they never really arrived   How they hid in the high trees

Mauka : ground-ache   turning to the mountains
The brother   sister so far from home   Look —
          each tree is moving   splitting their silver leaves in the wind

                    the tiered banyan   the fireheads   the bamboo
                    stalk and stalk and no clear view
                    What we want is a flood   a whole coursing   rushing

the valley flushed
the cement turned up   and Mānoa awash with living water

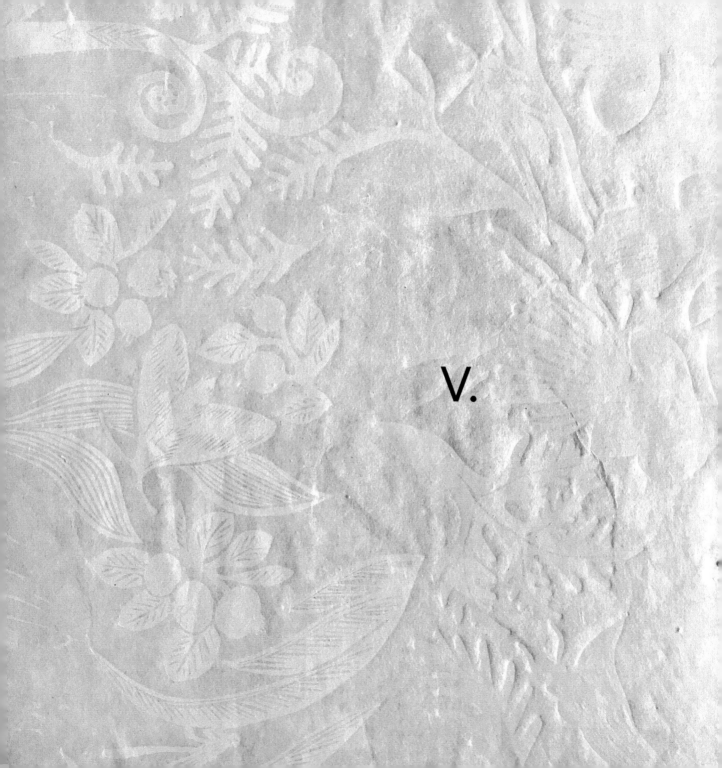

V.

ALL WE KNOW IS THE SUMMIT:

Notes on "Invoking the Bodhisattvas' Names in Honolulu"

Invoking the names of Bodhisattvas is a Buddhist practice that involves calling upon specific Bodhisattvas for help and guidance. At our Buddhist temple in Kapālama, we call them by their Japanese names — Kannon, Yakushi Nyorai, Jizō, and others. Bodhisattvas are beings who have delayed Buddhahood to remain on earth and help all living beings. Stepping from the incense-filled temple hall onto busy School Street, I often wonder how these Bodhisattvas may manifest now, in this corner of Honolulu. And by what names should I call them? Sometimes, as I walk through my neighborhood in Kapālama, I catch sight of my 3rd and 4th grade poetry students as they walk home from school. And because our neighborhood can be dangerous, I say a small prayer,
                                                    wishing them safe passage
                                 under the grace of a Bodhisattva.

My home was not always the highly urbanized place that it is today. Looking back through the layers of history laid upon this land, there are other stories. The city of Honolulu was originally understood as a collection of ahupua'a — watershed land divisions that stretch from mountain peak to ocean reef. The ahupua'a where I live is Kapālama — a narrow stretch of land between the larger valleys of Nu'uanu and Kalihi. Kapālama is fed by two streams (the lifeforce of any ahupua'a): Niuhelewai and Kapālama stream. From pre-contact Hawai'i up until the early 1900's, these streams watered a floodplain that was cultivated by Native Hawaiian families into lo'i fields for the farming of kalo (taro). Old pictures show thatched houses amongst the gardens and land surveys reveal an extensive system of aqueducts. John Papa 'Ī'ī writes of the abundance of the area in the 1860's: "When the trail reached the bridge, it began going along the banks of taro patches, up to the other side of Kapālama, to the plain of Kaiwi'ula on to the taro patches, on into Kahauiki and up to the other side…"

On the other side is the ahupua'a of Kalihi. In 1817, Otto von Kotzebue described Kalihi as a "beautifully cultivated valley, which is bounded towards the north by romantic scenery of woody mountains, and on the south by the sea." Kalihi, too, was full of lo'i fields — a series of step-like paddies with shallow water and rich mud. Von Kotzebue writes, "In the spaces between the fields, which are from three to six feet broad, there are very pleasant shady avenues, and on both sides bananas and sugar cane are planted." The broad green valley of Kalihi is now bisected by a highway. The fertile plains hold housing projects, warehouses, strip malls, and fields of concrete. Kapālama is often conflated with Kalihi in people's minds and in the area's popular name: "Kalihi-Palama."

In the noise of the city,
                          it is sometimes hard to remember the whole story.

Kapālama, although a small ahupua'a, became well-known when King Kamehameha I began farming the area in the early 19th century. His presence on the land was significant; after a period of warfare during unification, King Kamehameha I encouraged his people to return to farming and build stability. Historian Samuel Kamakau notes: "After the pestilence had subsided, the chiefs again took up farming, and Kamehameha cultivated land at Waikiki, Honolulu, and Kapalama and fed the people." The "pestilence" that Kamakau references is the ruthless series of diseases introduced to the islands by foreign explorers, missionaries, and mercenaries. According to R.D.K. Herman, "Following 'the venereals' introduced by early explorers, epidemics of mumps, smallpox, measles, influenza, and dysentery swept through the islands, affecting primarily the immunologically unprotected Native Hawaiians."

          These diseases, cumulatively, resulted in the death of 70-90%
          of the Native Hawaiian population.

The social and cultural disruption that accompanied this rapid depopulation was one of the factors that intensified the effects of western imperialism and, ultimately, facilitated the illegal overthrow of the Hawaiian kingdom in 1893.

Hansen's disease, then known as leprosy or ma'i lepera, was one of the most significant and long-lasting outbreaks to hit Hawai'i. Between 1865 and 1900, more that 5,000 people, ninety percent of whom where Native Hawaiian, were diagnosed with leprosy and isolated from their families. Suspected lepers were often arrested and sent to the Kalihi Leprosy Hospital to await sentencing. R.D.K. Herman writes, "The verdict of the examining board ('clean,' 'suspect,' or 'leper') determined whether or not a person was to be sent to the leper settlement 'to remain there until they die.'" This leper settlement was located on the remote Makanalua penninsula on the island of Molokai. Children were separated from their parents, spouses from their partners — the disease torn families and communities apart. The spread of this sickness also fueled western discourses on Hawaiian vulnerability to disease and associates with filth and sin (which missionaries insisted were related to illness). Kerri Inglis writes, "The stigma leprosy derived from the Western/Judeo-Christian tradition is a strong and negative one. Adding to this stigma were foreign preceptions that Hawaiian culture was uncivilized, immoral, and lascivious." These rhetorical frames served white supremacist and imperialist desires within Hawaiʻi and internationally.

Hansen's disease was just one of many factors that contributed to intense Native Hawaiian depopulation, from more than 800,000 in 1778 to 37,635 in 1900. During this period of sickness and cultural upheaval, thousands of laborers from Asia and elsewhere arrived in the Hawaiian islands. Beginning in the 1850's, immigrants from China, Japan, Portugal, Okinawa, Korea, the Philippines, and Puerto Rico arrived to work in sugarcane and pineapple plantations. Eventually, they made their homes in Kalihi, Kapālama, Liliha and other neighborhoods in Honolulu. Many of these immigrant groups were a part of the rapid urbanization and Americanization of the islands. The American dream continues to be a powerful force in the islands, even as we experience the abuses of multinational corporations, problems with houselessness, drug epidemics, and environmental degradation. Kalihi and Kapālama are now home to the most recent waves of immigrants to Oʻahu: those from Pacific Islands and the Philippines. In an economy where over half of the families in Hawaiʻi struggle to make ends meet, we have become familiar with the way things are. All we know is the summit, this city full of concrete and asphalt.

And yet, these islands remind us that this isn't the way things always were or have to be.

FURTHER

For an in-depth biography of John Papa ʻĪʻī, see Marie Alohalani Brown's book, *Facing the Spears of Change: the life and legacy of John Papa ʻĪʻī.*

Information on the history of Hawaiʻi by John Papa ʻĪʻī and Samuel Kamakau, along with maps and details on Kapālama and Kalihi were found in a cultural survey conducted for the Honolulu Authority for Rapid Transit (HART).

For more on Joseph Kahahawai, see *Local Story: The Massie-Kahahawai Case and the Culture of History* by John Rosa.

For more on disease and leprosy in Hawaiʻi, see Kerri Inglis's book *Maʻi Lepera* and R. D. K. Herman's article "Out of Sight, Out of Mind, Out of Power: Leprosy, Race, and Colonization in Hawaiʻi," published in *Hūlili* Vol. 6 (2010) and available online.

For more on the difficult economic realities of living in Hawaiʻi, see Hawaiʻi Business Magazine's article, "Half of Hawaiʻi Barely Gets By."

THERE WERE STORIES AT WORK IN US:

Notes on "Mānoa"

In elementary school, I learned about the weather patterns of Mānoa Valley through the story of Kauawaʻahila, the brother cliff rain, and Kauakiʻowao, the sister mist and windy rain. I learned geology through stories of the goddess Pele, whose home is the volcano crater, Halemaʻumaʻu. In many ways, Hawaiian epistemology was integrated into my education.

> Yet, out on the playground,
> a mash-up of ghost stories roamed wild
> through our imaginations.

There were stories of Japanese *obake* without faces or feet. There were stories of ghosts that crouched on your chest as you slept. There were stories of night marchers — long lines of Hawaiian warrior spirits who would walk the old paths at night. We never knew just what to believe. Many of these stories had no cultural context for us and quickly moved into the realm of urban legend.

Mary Kawena Pukui tells a more complete version of the night marchers story with enough background to begin to understand its significance.

> Every Hawaiian has heard of the "Marchers of the Night," *ka huakaʻi o ka Pō*. A few have seen the procession. It is said that such sight is fatal unless one had a relative among the dead to intercede for him. If a man is found stricken by the roadside, a white doctor will pronounce the cause as heart failure, but a Hawaiian will think at once of the fatal night march.

She goes on to describe the nature of the different types of night marches: those for deceased chiefs and those for gods. The ghostly marchers carried kukui nut torches and great food calabashes. Sometimes there would be music and sometimes silence, depending on the chiefs' preferences in life. The marches of the gods were accompanied by whirlwinds or thunder and lightning. And anyone who looked on these marches would be struck dead unless they had a relative to claim and protect them. While these details sound just as terrifying as my childhood nightmares, Pukui adds the story of Mrs. Emma Akana Olmsted. She, too, grew up with stories of these marches and was afraid, but as an adult, she began to hear the marches for herself — "Beautiful loud chanting voices, the high notes of the flute and drumming so loud that it seems beaten upon the side of the house beside her bed. The voices are so distinct that if she could write music she would be able to set down the notes they sang."

In this context,
>   the marchers of the night are beautiful reminders
>   of those who have passed
>   and their continued presence in our lives today.

FURTHER

A full reprint of Mary Kawena Pukui's story "The Marchers of the Night" may be found in *A Hawai'i Anthology* edited by Joseph Stanton.

THERE IS A WAR:

Notes on "War Games"

It is a daily occurrence: warplanes dart overhead, artillery fire echoes across the valley, battleships crowd our horizons. These are just war games, we are told, training exercises for the U.S. military. As of 2007, the military controls more than 5% of the total land in Hawai'i, including 22.4% of land on the island of O'ahu. Hawai'i is one of the most highly militarized places in the world and the headquarters of the US Pacific Command and Fleet. Writer and activist, Haunani-Kay Trask succinctly describes the role of these forces, "Shiploads and planeloads of American military forces continue to pass through Hawai'i on their way to imperialist wars in Asia and elsewhere... Hawai'i is a militarized outpost of empire, deploying troops and nuclear ships to the south and east to prevent any nation's independence from American domination."

How did Hawai'i come to be so completely occupied
by a foreign military in land, institution, and mind?

Perhaps it began when two members of the U.S. military visited the Kingdom of Hawai'i in 1873 disguised as tourists. General Schofield and Lieutenant Colonel Alexander were on a secret mission to survey the islands for potential naval ports. When they set eyes on Pu'uloa, they reported back to their superiors: "It is the key to the Central Pacific Ocean, it is the gem of these islands." From a military standpoint, Hawai'i was strategically located as a potential refilling station and base from which to control the Pacific and Asia. Understanding the U.S. military's desire for a port, a haole (white/foreign) minority in Honolulu used Pu'uloa as a bargaining piece in their machinations for power. These white sugar barons, business men, and lawyers, many of whom were Hawai'i-born children of American missionaries, formed the "Missionary party." In order to secure a better trade deal for Hawai'i-grown sugar and amass more wealth, members of the Missionary party advocated for the 1875 Treaty of Reciprocity and its later extension which granted lands in Pu'uloa to the U.S. military. This same party used an armed militia to intimidate King Kalākaua into signing the 1887 Constitution of the Hawaiian Kingdom, known as the

"Bayonet Constitution." This constitution stripped the monarchy of authority and was widely contested by Hawaiian leaders and subjects of the Kingdom.

When Queen Lili'uokalani, King Kalākaua's sister and successor, tried to enact a new constitution that would restore Native Hawaiian political power, the Missionary party conspired with U.S. foreign minister John Stevens and Captain G.C. Wiltse to stage a coup d'état. The Missionary party, led by Lorrin Thurston, convinced Minister Stevens to land American troops from the armed warship, USS Boston, in support of their new government. On January 16th, 1893, one hundred and sixty-two sailors and marines landed illegally in Honolulu. Donning military coats and carrying rifles, the soldiers marched through the streets, falling into rank and file at the Arlington Hotel grounds. With the force of the U.S. military backing them, Lorrin Thurston and others of the Missionary party declared a new provisional government,
deposing the Queen.

That there was a treaty of perpetual amity between the Kingdom of Hawai'i and the U.S., that Hawai'i was a recognized member of the family of nations since 1843, and that it is illegal under international law to invade a recognized sovereign nation, were all points that Queen Lili'uokalani emphasized in her protests. Using her impressive knowledge of the law, Queen Lili'uokalani submitted formal protests to U.S. President Cleveland and the provisional government in Honolulu. President Cleveland ordered an investigation of the matter and later issued a statement condemning the actions of U.S. foreign minister Stevens and calling for the provisional government to step down. However, President Cleveland lacked the political ability to enforce the restoration of the monarchy. He was succeeded by President McKinley who, along with congress, used the outbreak of the Spanish-American war as an excuse to issue a joint resolution, annexing Hawai'i.

The years after annexation saw a rapid militarization of the islands.

Kyle Kajihiro writes, "U.S. occupation ushered in a period of unprecedented military expansion in Hawai'i. Construction of a naval base at Pearl Harbor began in 1900, and it was soon followed by Fort Shafter, Fort Ruger, Fort Armstrong, Fort DeRussy, Fort Kamehameha, Fort Weaver, and Schofield Barracks. Brigadier General Montgomery M. Macomb, commander of the U.S. Army, Pacific [sic] stated, 'Oahu is to be encircled with a ring of steel.'" At the time of annexation, the U.S. seized control of nearly 1.8 million acres of former national and "crown lands" belonging to the Kingdom of Hawai'i. Much of this land was claimed by the military or later leased by the State of Hawai'i to the military for a pittance each year.

> Over the years, the U.S. military has committed countless abuses to the water, land, flora, and fauna of the islands.

The island of Kaho'olawe was so heavily bombed by the U.S. military that the explosions cracked the water table. Bombing in Mākua valley on the leeward side of O'ahu left craters (now filled with contaminated water). Unexploded ordinances still lurk in bays and valleys across the islands. And although the U.S. military signed contracts guaranteeing that the affected areas would be cleaned and restored to their former state, there are places where leftover chemicals and explosives make it too dangerous to set foot on the land.

FURTHER

For more on militarization, see Kyle Kajihiro's essay "The Militarizing of Hawai'i," in *Asian Settler Colonialism: for Local Governance to the Habits of Everyday Life in Hawai'i* and his article "Nation Under the Gun: Militarism and Resistance in Hawai'i" found in Cultural Survival Quarterly Magazine.

For more on Native Hawaiian resistance, see *From a Native Daughter: Colonialism and Sovereignty in Hawai'i* by Haunani-Kay Trask and *Aloha Betrayed: Native Hawaiian Resistance to American Colonialism* by Noenoe K. Silva.

A nuanced account of the illegal overthrow can be found in *Hawaii's Story by Hawaii's Queen*, written by Queen Lili'uokalani and *Dismembering Lahui: a history of the Hawaiian nation to 1887* by Jonathan Kamakawiwo'ole Osorio.

For more information on Mākua valley, visit: www.malamamakua.org.

WHERE OUR GRANDPARENTS SANG:

Notes on "Driving to the North Shore, I Imagine My Brother"

My great-grandparents came to Hawaiʻi from Hiroshima, Japan in the early 1900's. My great-grandfathers came first as laborers to work in the sugarcane plantations. When they had saved enough, they brought over their wives and children to begin a life here. Great-Grandfather Uejio opened a confectionery shop in Hilo and Great-Grandfather Nakanishi trained as a carpenter in Honolulu. My family became a part of the booming population of Japanese in Hawaiʻi — a full one-third of the total population by 1900.

Japanese had originally been recruited to fuel the sugarcane industry's demands for cheap labor. In 1881, King Kalākaua visited Japanese Emperor Meiji on his world tour; the resulting diplomatic relationship between leaders increased recruitment and bettered contract conditions for Japanese laborers. Despite these improved conditions, life on the sugarcane plantations was difficult. Workers were paid under $10 a month for long days of labor. Both men and women from many different ethnic groups (Chinese, Japanese, Korean, Okinawan, Puerto Rican, Filipino, and, in a supervisory role, Portuguese) cut cane, trimmed leaves, and sweated together in the sugarcane fields. In order to make the time pass more quickly, some of the Japanese workers sang hole hole bushi — folk songs that reflected the everyday trails of the plantation:

> *"Kane wa kachiken / Washa horehoreyo / Ase to namida no / Tomokasegi.*
> My husband cuts the cane stalks, / And I trim the leaves, /
> With sweat and tears we both work, / For our means."

When many Japanese and other Asians came to Hawaiʻi, they entered into a fraught political situation. At this time, the Kingdom of Hawaiʻi had just been overthrown and a new territorial leadership was working to assert control. Because Japanese made up such a large percentage of the population — reaching 40% by 1924 — the Territorial leadership was worried that Japanese might take over Hawaiʻi. While first generation immigrants to the Territory of Hawaiʻi could not vote or own property, their children, who were born in the Territory, would be afforded those rights. Haole elite, along with racist nativist groups on the continent, agitated to ban Japanese laborers. They succeeded in 1908 with the "Gentleman's Agreement," which stopped all immigration, save for immediate family members of workers already in Hawaiʻi. In 1924, the

United States instituted the exclusionary Immigration Act, which banned all immigration from Asia.

Nonetheless, my grandparents were born into a large Japanese community in the Territory of Hawai'i, which itself was an occupying force in the Kingdom of Hawai'i. While my great-grandparents always wished to return to Japan, the only home my grandparents knew was Hawai'i. My grandfather worked at Musashiya Dry Goods store and my grandmother was a secretary for the psychologist, Dr. Haertig. And while over 50% of first-generation Japanese returned to Japan or moved on to the West Coast of the American continent, the majority of my family stayed in Hawai'i.

I live in the house that my great-grandfather built.

The house is almost 100 years old and has been a refuge for our family, providing shelter and stability for generations. It was the first Japanese house built in this area of Kapālama. My great-grandfather encouraged other Japanese families to move in, and soon a neighborhood formed. Now our neighbors are Chinese, Filipino, Japanese, and haole. The only Hawaiian family on my block lives in a small apartment build into the basement of our haole neighbor's house. According to David Stannard, "Hawaiians represent roughly 20 percent of the state's population, but they occupy less than 10 percent of the housing units in the islands." Data from the Native Hawaiian Data Book shows that Native Hawaiian families suffer the highest rates of poverty and health outcomes and the lowest rates of education. Native Hawaiians are disproportionately represented in carceral systems — partially due to harsher treatment by the court systems.

This is the story that I did not hear as a child:
while my ancestors worked hard and sacrificed for our family, Native Hawaiians faced cultural erasure and systemic disenfranchisement. And while Hawai'i-born Japanese fought in WWII, returned with the GI Bill, and rose to positions of power in education, business, and government,
            Native Hawaiians have been fighting for sovereignty.

Growing up, I believed that I had been born in the State of Hawai'i, a state of the United States of America. And while this is true in some respects, it is also true that I was born into the illegally occupied Kingdom of Hawai'i — a nation that continues to exist despite American domination. The 1993 Apology Bill passed by the U.S. Congress, acknowledges that "the indigenous Hawaiian people have never directly relinquished their inherent sovereignty as a people or over their national lands to the United States, either through their monarchy or through a plebiscite or referendum." This means that Native Hawaiians have a strong claim on the restoration of their sovereignty.

What do I do now, living in this contentious place?
            And how can I take responsibility for the legacies that I've inherited?

FURTHER

For démographic information on Japanese in Hawai'i, see *A Pictorial History of the Japanese in Hawaii* by Odo and Sinoto, and "The Japanese in Hawaii: a historical and demographic perspective" by Eleanor C. Nordyke and Y. Scott Matsumoto.

For more on plantations in Hawai'i, including information on immigration and hole hole bushi, see *Pau Hana: Plantation Life and Labor in Hawaii* by Ronald Takaki.

For Native Hawaiian carceral and health information, see "A Nation Incarcerated" by Healani Sonoda and "The Hawaiians: Health, Justice, and Sovereignty" by David Stannard featured in *Asian Settler Colonialism: for Local Governance to the Habits of Everyday Life in Hawai'i.*

For more on the legal history of Hawai'i, including the contested nature of its statehood today, see *Ua Mau Ke Ea Sovereignty Endures* by David Keanu Sai.

PLACE OF REFUGE

Notes on "Waimea Valley"

Waimea Valley on Oʻahu is a *puʻuhonua* (place of refuge) that holds a long association with the Kahuna Nui class. Kāhuna were experts in their chosen fields, including navigation, astronomy, medicine, fishing, canoe building, prophesy, and agriculture (among others). Waimea Valley was home to the renown prophet Kaʻopulupulu and Hewahewa, spiritual advisor to King Kamehameha I. In addition to kāhuna, makaʻāinana (common citizens) also lived in Waimea Valley and farmed a lush abundance of sweet potatoes, yams, sugarcane, kalo, breadfruit, banana, and ʻawa.

> The plentiful and rich red waters of Waimea Valley
> made it a place of great wealth.

Waimea Valley was the first place on Oʻahu where Captain Cook's ships landed in 1779. This initial contact, compounded with others, eventually led to an abusive sandalwood trade. The forests of Waimea Valley and the surround hillsides were denuded. Without a healthy forest to absorb and buffer the rains, they coursed through the valley, causing a huge flood in 1898. After this flood, most of the Hawaiian families living in the valley left to settle in other ahupuaʻa.

After the Māhele in 1848, a process that privitized land, Waimea Valley changed hands multiple times. By the early 1900's, the Castle & Cook pineapple and sugar company had taken over Waimea Valley for the use of ranching and farming. In the 1960's, the Waimea Falls Ranch and Stables corporation bought the valley to serve the rising tourist market. At its height, in the 1960's and 1970's, there were guided tours, hula and cliff-diving shows, and 75-cent stagecoach rides with actors who played cowboys and Indians. Waimea Falls Ranch and Stables turned into Waimea Falls Adventure Park and would have been furthered developed by private owners had not a coalition of individuals and organizations worked together to buy the land for conservation and education. Now Waimea Valley is owned and stewarded by the Native Hawaiian non-profit, Hiʻipaka LLC.

Over a thousand people visit the park each day. They walk through the botanical gardens, visit the archeological sites, and swim in the pool below Waihī falls. There is a paved road all the way up to the waterfall, trafficked by carts and throngs of visitors. There are also pavilions, informational placards, a gift shop, and restaurants.

> Yet,
> the developed reality of Waimea Valley does not erase
> its past or continued sense of sacredness.

Everywhere in the valley are old stone walls and the foundations of houses from before the time of Captain Cook. The ridge cliffs are home to countless burial sites — the bones watching over the valley from their secret caves. Remarking on what makes Waimea Valley special, Margaret Kaʻulaʻaihawane Berke Chun writes, "Maybe because of the sense of isolation, the sense of quietness, the sense of beauty. Because even today, you know, those of us who have been to the Valley, and have been here even for just a little while —
you become connected with it."

FURTHER

For more legends, history, and archeological information associated with Waimea Valley, see *Waimea Valley, Oʻahu: A Cultural and Archeological Assessment* and *The History of Waimea Valley, Oʻahu* by Anne Takemoto.

For more on the anthropology and mythology of Oʻahu, see *Sites of Oahu* by Elspeth Sterling and Catherine Summers.

For more on the history of Waimea valley, important cultural sites, and its botanical gardens, visit: www.waimeavalley.net. Much of the history and cultural understanding expressed in these notes and the Waimea Valley poems are thanks to Ah Lan Kaʻulameialani Diamond, Cultural Programs Manager at Waimea Valley.

HIS STRUGGLES HAD MANY ARMS

Notes on "The Shark"

The cultural and geographic tapestry of Hawai'i is woven by stories. There are stories everywhere, kept in stone and spring and mountain peak. Wahi pana (storied places) link the land with narrative. By moving physically through the islands one is also moving through a vast, interwoven text. Ku'ualoha Ho'omanawanui emphasizes the distinctions between Native Hawaiian and Western storytelling, "In Hawaiian culture the telling of mo'olelo is important because of the different emphasis on place than that found in Western tales. For examples, Hawaiian wahi pana stresses the storyteller's knowledge of a place, which is revealed in the detailed setting of the mo'olelo. The 'āina was not merely a setting or backdrop, but an integral part of the plot."

> The 'āina (the living earth)
> is a central element of all stories, as it is central to all life.

Maya Kawailanaokeawaiki Saffery, emphasizes this kanaka-'āina (human-land) connection: "Preserving and then passing down living narratives from one generation to the next have been part of our tradition as Kānaka since our origins. Whether they take the form of mele (poetry, song, chants) composed and performed, or of mo'olelo (stories, histories) told and retold first orally and then in written form, many of these histories focus on the kanaka-'āina connection because it is this relationship that ultimately defines us as a people and allows us to live a pono (balanced, sustained, nourished) life." Some stories are secret and not to be shared, some have been passed on through family lines, and some are woven into the Hawaiian language itself.

There is an 'ōlelo no'eau (proverb) that states:
> "E ao o pau po'o, pau hi'u ia manō"
> (Be careful lest you go head and tail into the shark).

This proverb is one of many collected and recorded by Mary Kawena Pukui. According to Pukui, this phrase was "a warning to be on one's guard." She explains, "Nanaue, of Waipi'o, had two forms — that of a man and that of a shark. As people passed his farm to go to the beach, he would utter this warning. After they had passed, he would run to the river, change into a shark, and swim under the water to the sea where he would catch and eat those he had warned. No one knew that it was Nanaue who was eating the people until someone pulled off the shoulder-covering he always wore and discovered a shark's mouth between his shoulder blades. After he was put to death the people were safe again."

> The story of Nanaue has been told and retold
>   for generations
>   ever since the events took place during the
>   reign of 'Umi in the 16th century.

Emma M. Nakuina wrote and published an English version of Nanaue's story in 1893. In it, she describes the meeting of Nanaue's human mother with the shark god Kamohaoli'i. Their son, Nanaue, was half-shark and grew up in Waipi'o Valley with certain strict rules: he was to always wear a shoulder-covering to hide the shark jaw on his back and he was forbidden from eating meat. One day, when Nanaue's parents were not around, the boy's grandfather gave him some pig meat to eat. The taste awakened a ravenous and blood-thirsty nature in the boy. When he grew older, Nanaue began to secretly eat his neighbors.

This story is recorded in the land itself — at the mouth of the Waipi'o River where Nanaue fled after his true identity was revealed. The story continues on the island of Molokai, where the marks of Nanaue's struggle against his captors are gouged into Pu'u-manō hill. There is a rock called Kainalu which is still grooved with the indentations of the ropes that held the net that finally caught Nanaue.

Living in the presence of wahi pana and the stories that they hold, I have found that my sense of the possible is expanded. When I first read Emma M. Nakuina's version of the Nanaue story, I became fascinated with the idea of manō-kānaka (shark-people). My poem, "The Shark" is a contemporary imagining of the story of Nanaue. The poem does not attempt to follow the plot line of the original tale or the details of the geographic and cultural landscape, instead it fixates on certain emotional moments from the story. Inter-species love between a woman and a shark, the birth of a half-shark son, and the horror of this son's ruthless and blood-thirsty nature are all woven into the poem. This poem imagines a mother's point of view and asks:

> How do we come to terms with our "fearful offspring"?

FURTHER

For kuʻualoha hoʻomanawanui's complete essay see, "This Land is Your Land, This Land Was My Land" in *Asian Settler Colonialism: from local governance to the habits of everyday life in Hawaiʻi.*

For more on stories and metaphor see *Kanaka ʻŌiwi Methodologies* including Maya Kawailanaokeawaiki Saffery's essay, "He Ala Nihinihi Ia A Hiki I Ka Mole: A Precarious Yet Worthwhile Path to Kuleana Through Hawaiian Place-Based Education."

For more ʻōlelo noʻeau see Mary Kawena Pukui's *ʻŌlelo Noʻeau: Hawaiian Proverbs and Poetical Sayings.*

For more on manō-kānaka, see Emma M. Nakuina's "Nanaue" and Dennis Kawaharada's literary notes in *Hawaiian Fishing Traditions* by Moke Manu and Others. Final quoted text is from Emma M. Nakuina's "Nanaue."

SHORT NOTES

On "The Pacific Nalakah"
The Pacific Nalakah is an imaginary animal.

On "Mānoa" (3)
With gratitude and admiration, the line "Stand right there, be my foreground" was borrowed from Prageeta Sharma's poem "Be My Foreground" published in *Infamous Landscapes*.

On "Mixed"
The form and content of this poem were inspired by Arthur Rimbaud's "Bad Blood," from *A Season in Hell*.

On "Bitterroots"
With gratitude and admiration, the line "All things move faster than time and make a stillness thereby" was borrowed from Linda Gregg's poem "Praising Spring" published in *Alma*. The poem also carries echoes of form and focus from Gregg's "We Manage Most When We Manage Small" from *Too Bright to See*.

On "Given"
The "culture-related syndromes" alluded to in this poem ("fire-illness," *hikikomori, and "sudden limb loss"*) are referenced in Frank Bures's article "A Mind Dismembered: In Search of the Magical Penis Thieves," originally published in *Harper's Magazine* in 2008.

On "Three Views of O'ahu"
The form of this poem was inspired by Janine Oshiro's poem "Three Bays" published in *Pier*.

On "Waikīkī Diptych"
The photos of albatross referenced in this poem come from Chris Jordan's work documenting baby albatross deaths on Midway Atoll. Of the project, he writes: "On Midway Atoll, a remote cluster of islands more than 2,000 miles from the nearest continent, the detritus of our mass consumption surfaces in an astonishing place: inside the stomachs of thousands of dead baby albatrosses. The nesting chicks are fed lethal quantities of plastic by their parents, who mistake the floating trash for food as they forage over the vast polluted Pacific Ocean."

On *"Elegy with Whale Song"*
This poem is dedicated to Eduardo Chirinos.

On *"Pacific Trash Vortex"*
Known as the "Great Pacific Garbage Patch" or "Pacific Trash Vortex," this huge swath of ocean is hemmed in by the North Pacific Subtropical Gyre — a circular current that has collected millions of pieces of floating plastic and microplastic trash. It is impossible to know how big this garbage patch is — scientists estimate between 270,000 square miles and 5,800,000 square miles (about the size of Russia). The garbage patch is not actually an island, but more of a soup of plastic pieces both large and small extending for many feet below the surface of the sea. There may also be a massive underwater trash heap forming beneath the garbage patch. For more, see the Smithsonian Institute's website on marine plastics.

On *"Portrait of my Brother as a Bulwer's Petrel"*
According to the online Hawaiian dictionary, wehewehe.org, the original Hawaiian name for the Bulwer's Petrel is ʻou. The dictionary describes the Bulwer's petrel as "a small sea bird; for some people, an ʻaumakua. Also [known as] ʻouʻou." Information about the Bulwer's Petrel and the small leeward island of Nihoa referenced in the poem comes from *Hawaii, A Natural History* by Sherwin Carlquist. This poem also modifies a line by Carlquist: "[Necker] is an island which extends far out to sea, as far as a bird can fly for feeding yet still return by nightfall."

On *"A Homecoming"*
This poem is written in the *zuihitsu* style and borrows formal elements from Sei Shonagon's *The Pillow Book*. The line "My students ask" echoes Eduardo Chirinos's poem "Love Poem with Dark Face."

On *"Mahalo ā Nui"*
This catalog of gratitude is indebted to Ross Gay's "Catalog of Unabashed Gratitude."

EVERYWHERE THE OCEAN

Notes on "Mānoa"

Mānoa
　　　　is a broad valley hemmed in
by sculpted green cliffs. The streams that flow through Mānoa
eventually find their way to the sea at Waikīkī —
　　　　　　　　　　linking these two (seemingly disparate) locations.

Sometimes a light rain falls over Waʻahila ridge on the eastern side of Mānoa
Valley. Sometimes a cold rain descends from the valley head, misty and riding
the winds. In stories, these weather patterns are children: Kauawaʻahila and
Kauakiʻowao, twins who ran away from home. The twins were beautiful and
beloved. Their home was Mt. Kaʻala. And though their mother died, they were
happy with their father, Chief Kakaʻakea. However, their new stepmother
was cruel. When their father went away to the island of Hawaiʻi, the abuse
became so bad that they ran away to Mānoa Valley and hid in the high forests
of Kōnāhuanui. Their stepmother, Hawea, went searching for the children,
following the rainbows that often appeared wherever the twins went. She
found them at Kōnāhuanui, so they ran again, hiding near the valley entrance,
then in caves near Kūkaʻoʻo heiau. She found them again and again they ran,
hiding and foraging for food. Finally, they found shelter in a rocky cave near
ʻUalakaʻa hill. And, search as she did, Hawea could not find the children.

　　　　　　　　　　　　　We still watch the twin rains
　　　　　　　　　　　　　run across the valley,
　　　　　　　　　　　　　accompanied by rainbows.

The rain that falls over Mānoa valley runs through gutters, over concrete,
into drainages, and eventually empties into the Ala Wai Canal. In my lifetime,
I've only ever known the Ala Wai to be fetid and polluted, and Waikīkī to
be overrun with tall buildings. Yet, in my great-grandmother's generation,
Waikīkī's name made sense — the stretch of beach was backed by a lush
marshland where fresh water spouted and fed the twisting streams. There
were fishponds, kalo, rice paddies, duck ponds, and a wild abundance of sea life.
The children who lived in Waikīkī would swim until their dark hair bleached
blond in the salt water. They paddled surfboards up the streams, exploring the
waterways. They caught pipipi, manini and mullet. They picked limu near the

shoreline. Doveline "Tootsie" Notley Steer remembers the seasons for fishing in the wide bay:

> "Oh, I'm telling you.
> > When the crabs, the big white crabs, would come...
> > > they would come in by the thousands.

So we would line up the beach and would have these long sheets and when the wave brings them in, we'd scoop it and roll the crabs on the dry part up the shore." Lobster, shrimp, fish, crab, and limu thrived in Waikīkī's estuary where Mānoa's streams emptied into the ocean. Fumiko Nunotani remembers the reef that stretched the length of Waikīkī:

> "You can walk miles and miles out
> > and only get one shallow wave that used to come in.
> But now you don't have that because they took off the corals."

In 1921, the State of Hawai'i began construction on the Ala Wai Canal to drain Waikīkī marsh of its many waterways, mud plains, and fish ponds. The construction project took seven years to complete and resulted in a spit of land so heavy developed by the tourism industry that it is difficult to imagine Waikīkī as it was, with spouting (kīkī) fresh water (wai). After the Ala Wai Canal was completed, the marsh was filled in with dirt and coral.

Soon enough, other construction projects began — hotels and homes, Fort DeRussy military base, and a corresponding channel cut through the reef to bring in a 69-ton artillery gun. These changes ushered in an age of erosion that continues to this day. To build up the beach, barges of sand were gouged from Waimea Bay and other beaches in Hawai'i and, along with more sand shipped from Australia, dumped onto Waikīkī. Most recently, beach "replenishment projects" pump sand from the sea beds offshore with the use of giant pipes.

> Yet,
> the waves still break over the seawalls
> > and salt water sloshes up storm gutters at high tide.

Rising sea levels and eroding beaches do not stop the tourists from coming. In 2018, nearly 10 million tourists visited Hawai'i. With a total resident population of only 1.42 million, tourism often dominates life in the islands. The resulting paradigm makes it difficult to see past the duration of a vacation. The weather must be sunny, the food plentiful, and the hotels luxurious; everything is ringed with the expectation of perfection for those 5-10 vacation days. Yet, as a resident, the vacations never end here. It is either high season or higher season and we cannot keep up.

> While multinational corporations rake in millions of dollars, the land, infrastructure, and people of Hawai'i suffer.

Simultaneously, people around the world are being sold a fake version of Hawai'i that feeds into the corporate tourism industry. As the Lonely Planet states in their description of O'ahu, "The island was one of the first to implant itself in the world's collective longing for a tropical vacation, thanks to the success of Waikiki." The myths of paradisiacal beaches and colorful local culture continue to draw visitors. The Lonely Planet continues on, "Many come for the Waikiki vacation package, and all are pleasantly surprised by what lies beyond the hotel. A short distance away are dramatic mountain ranges, aqua-blue coral bays and wide sandy beaches. There's snorkeling in the old volcanic crater of Hanauma Bay, monster waves at the surfing haven of the North Shore, genuine Hawaiian ukulele bands, hiking through tropical forests and a general aloha spirit."

> In the machine of the tourism industry, mountains, beaches, bays, and people
>
> have been packaged for tourist consumption.

Words like aloha have been plucked from their cultural contexts and printed onto T-shirts, bags, and signs to sell a feeling of warmth, relaxation, and the exotic. These associations belay the depth of aloha. Malcolm Nāea Chun explains, "...aloha is special because it upholds, reaffirms, and binds relationships. Aloha should not be taken lightly. It should not be used casually or frivolously."

Nana Veary reaffirms this idea, "The word [aloha] is imbued with a great deal of power. I do not use the word casually. Aloha is a feeling, a recognition of the divine. It is not just a word or greeting. When you say 'aloha' to someone, you are conveying or bestowing this feeling." Understanding aloha at such depths can be life-changing. M. Kamana'o'i'o Kim Jr. talks about living into this ethos of aloha, "You have aloha for all things, for everything around you, and that has been a 180-degree huli (turn) for me. You got to have aloha for the ʻāina, for the air, for the wind. And, you have got to have aloha for the kūpuna."

From these kūpuna (elders) and from the work of poets like Imaikalani Kalahele, Mahealani Perez Wendt, and Wayne Kaumauliʻi Westlake, among others, I am learning more about the secret words — those words that move past the tourist veneer. These writers and thinkers have shown me the ways that our human lives connect with the natural world. It is what Buddhists call "reverence for life," and what Nana Veary describes as "living and becoming a part of everything around you. This is what metaphysics teaches and how the Hawaiians lived."

FURTHER

To hear more stories about old Hawaiʻi visit the University of Hawaiʻi's Center for Oral History.

Information on "replenishment projects" and the erosion of Waikīkī beach may be found in the Honolulu Star Advertiser and Honolulu Magazine.

For more on aloha, see Malcolm Nāea Chun's *No Nā Mamo: traditional and contemporary Hawaiian beliefs and practices* and Nana Veary's *Change We Must*.

For a complete telling of the story of Kauawaʻahila and Kauakiʻowao, see the Hawaiian language newspaper *Kuokoa*, Nov. 26, 1915

With gratitude and admiration, "Mānoa"(V) incorporates text from the following poems:

Imaikalani Kalahele's poem "Make Rope," from *Kalahele*: "...putting one more / strand of coconut fiber / on to the kaula / he make one / fast twist..."

Mahealani Perez Wendt's poem "Blue Light," from *Uluhaimalama*: "His heart sang / For this boy's reward: / The green world below, / The blue light above."

Words from M. Kamanaʻoʻiʻo Kim Jr., published in *Hūlili Magazine* Vol.7 (2011), "Nā Hulu Kūpuna: Living and Sharing Hawaiian Wisdom" (available online).

And inspiration from Wayne Kaumauliʻi Westlake's poetry, especially "Down on the Sidewalk in Waikiki."

ACKNOWLEDGEMENTS

A heart full of gratitude to my parents, Jenny Wallace and Blake Nakanishi, to my grandparents, family, and ancestors. Thank you to my teachers, especially Eduardo Chirinos, Julie Marie Wade, Mary Szybist, Joanna Klink, Campbell McGrath, John Wat, Pat Takeshita, and Lisa Nagata. Thank you to Jason Ellinwood, Dennis Kawaharada, and Candace Fujikane who offered valuable feedback on this book. Thank you to my friends, writing community, and to my Portland loves, Emily Krafft, Kyra Plume, and Ryan Comandich. Thank you to Tupelo press, especially to my wonderful editor Kristina Marie Darling, and to Carl Phillips for selecting the manuscript. And always, to my beloved partner, Alex Salinas-Nakanishi — thank you for today.

These poems have appeared, sometimes in different forms, in the following magazines:

Gulf Coast Journal: "War Games "
Black Warrior Review: "The Shark" (published as "Nanaue")
Western Humanities Review: "Living Away" (published as "A Note on a Vacant Bus Seat")
Hawaii Pacific Magazine: "Mixed"
Gravel Magazine: "Bitterroots" (published as "The Story in Seasons")
Thalia Magazine: "Catalog" (published as "Wilderness Catalog")
Montana Natural History Magazine: "The Sun Moving Across This Particular Earth"
Third Coast Magazine: "Given"
Hoot: "Place(less)ness"
Camas Magazine: "Pacific Trash Vortex" (published as "Debris")

The following poems appeared in the chapbook *Mānoa Makai*, selected by Kimiko Hahn as Epiphany Edition's 2013 winning chapbook:

"Mānoa" (1-3)
"The Pacific Nalakah" (published as "The Pacific Naluaka")
"Three Views of Hawaii"
"Waimea Valley" (1-4)
"Mānoa" (published as "Mānoa Makai")

Photo: Gen Fujitani

Laurel Nakanishi was born and raised on the island of Oʻahu, Hawaiʻi. Through her work as a writer and educator, she has lived in Montana, Nicaragua, and Japan. She has been fortunate to receive grants from the Fulbright Foundation, Japan-US Friendship Commission, and Wrolstad Foundation. Her poetry and essays have appeared in national literary magazines and a prize-winning chapbook, *Mānoa|Makai*. Laurel received her MFA in poetry from the University of Montana and her MFA in creative non-fiction from Florida International University. She lives with her family in Honolulu, Hawaiʻi.